M000112533

THE MONEY REVOLUTION
Applying Christian Principles
to Handling Your Money

THE MONEY REVOLUTION
Applying Christian Principles
to Handling Your Money

John Preston

Authentic

LONDON ● COLORADO SPRINGS ● HYDERABAD

Copyright © 2007 John Preston

13 12 11 10 09 08 07   7 6 5 4 3 2 1

First published 2007 by Authentic Media
9 Holdom Avenue, Bletchley, Milton Keynes, Bucks, MK1 1QR, UK
1820 Jet Stream Drive, Colorado Springs, CO 80921, USA
OM Authentic Media, Medchal Road, Jeedimetla Village,
Secunderabad 500 055, A.P., India.

www.authenticmedia.co.uk

Authentic Media is a division of IBS-STL UK., a company limited by guarantee
(registered charity no. 270162)

The right of John Preston to be identified as the author
of this work has been asserted by him in accordance
with the Copyright, Designs and Patents Act 1988.

All rights reserved.

No part of this publication may be reproduced,
stored in a retrieval system, or transmitted in any form or by any means,
electronic or mechanical, including photocopy, recording or otherwise,
without the prior permission of the publisher or a licence permitting restricted
copying. In the UK such licences are issued by the Copyright Licensing Agency,
90 Tottenham Court Road, London W1P 9HE.

Unless otherwise indicated, all Scripture quotations are from
the HOLY BIBLE, TODAY'S NEW INTERNATIONAL VERSION
© 2004 by the International Bible Society.
Used by permission of Hodder & Stoughton, a member of Hodder Headline Ltd.
'TNIV' is a registered trademark of the International Bible Society.

All rights reserved.

British Library Cataloguing in Publication Data.
A catalogue record for this book is available from the British Library.

ISBN-13 978-1-85078-754-9
ISBN-10 1-85078-754-9

Cover design by James Kessell for Scratch the Sky Ltd. (www.scratchthesky.com)
Print Management by Adare Carwin
Printed in Great Britain by J.H. Haynes & Co., Sparkford

Contents

Foreword

In speaking about money, I have referred to it as being like God's sheepdog; snapping at our heels until we turn in the right direction. Like it or not, we are faced with many decisions about money – how much to give, save and spend, decisions about lifestyle, homes, credit and debt. All of these decisions demonstrate the values that are important to us.

Joyful, generous giving as a priority from our income can be a clear demonstration of Christian faith and commitment. But this book challenges us to think more widely than that. Our spending and our saving are also expressions of our faith. Lifestyle choices, from major decisions such as cars, holidays and homes to the products we buy in the supermarket, all reveal something about our values and principles. Our motivations in saving, and how we approach issues of credit and debt are faith issues just as much as our giving.

The Gospels are full of teaching that relates to issues of money, wealth and possessions; teaching which we are challenged to apply to our day-to-day decisions about money. *The Money Revolution* provides sound principles to shape our thinking, each backed by a biblical framework. Your investment in reading this book will return dividends if it helps you express your faith and Christian values in your wider stewardship of the resources God has given you.

For all that we have comes from God. Our money, God's sheepdog, will continue to snap at our heels until we place our homes, our time, our gifts and our money under the direction of the Good Shepherd, Jesus Christ.

The Most. Revd. & Rt. Hon. Dr. John Sentamu
The Archbishop of York
Primate of England and Metropolitan

Introduction

There is a story told about some of the Vikings who were converting to Christianity in the seventh and eighth centuries. As they were baptized by immersion in Britain's rivers, many felt a dilemma. While they were profoundly taken with their newly acquired faith, they recognized that as occupiers of a foreign country they might have to engage in battle. As they went under the water, some kept their right arms above the water. They were saying, in effect, 'You can have all of me Lord, save for my sword arm. I need to keep ownership of that for myself – I may need it someday.'

While Christians in the twenty-first century don't need to keep their sword arms above the waters of baptism, there are many who metaphorically hold their wallets above the water. Martin Luther once said, 'There are three conversions necessary: the conversion of the heart, the mind and the purse.' Quite often, it seems, our financial affairs lag behind the rest of our discipleship.

There are a number of lies, distortions and deceptions which can prevent us from fully understanding what it means to submit all that we have and all that we are to God. 'After all, I've earned it.' 'I give generously to the church – the rest is surely mine.' 'The wealth I have is my reward from God for my commitment to him – it's mine to do with what I want.'

Three of the Gospels record Jesus encountering a rich man who asks Jesus what he needs to do to inherit eternal life. Jesus asks him whether he has kept the commandments relating to how we live in relation to other people, and the rich man tells him that he has indeed done so. Jesus identifies one thing lacking in the man's faith and challenges him to give away his wealth to the poor. As the young man walks away filled with sadness, Jesus observes, 'it is easier for a camel to go through the eye of a needle than for the rich to enter the kingdom of God' (Lk. 18:25).

While Jesus was telling a joke, he wasn't joking. It seems that the priorities in this man's life were his wealth and riches. It is quite possible that he had not considered that his use of money had anything to do with his love for God. When Jesus challenged him to give his money away, he was offering him the opportunity to demonstrate a love for his neighbour and a love for God. The young man's great sadness revealed the value he placed on his wealth and prosperity in this world.

The Gospels record the disciples being amazed at Jesus' words. Their culture would have been likely to attribute riches to God's blessing. As he so often does, Jesus turns our human perceptions upside down. Here he clearly shows how wealth can prevent us from putting our trust and dependence in God, and in his grace.

'But I'm not wealthy. I'm not rich,' many of us say. When challenged with a passage like this, it is easy to think of a politician, footballer or film star who has significantly greater wealth than we do. Surely they are the rich people who need to pay heed to Jesus' message. But, when we compare levels of wealth around the world, we discover that this passage challenges every UK citizen. An annual income of £5,000 would place you in the richest 13.5% of the world's population, while an income of £26,000 would give you a place among the richest 1% – and you would not even pay higher rate tax within the UK.

Most of us have disposable income left after paying for food, shelter and clothing, and so in comparative terms UK citizens are wealthy. What we do with that wealth is a faith or spiritual question facing each and every one of us who seek to follow Jesus' teachings.

This short book presents five simple principles to help us tackle this issue and manage our money based on Christian values. Most readers will probably be giving regularly to their local church, and the Money Revolution seeks to enable a broader reflection on the subject of money from a Christian perspective. All too often the church talks about money only when it needs some more, rather than equipping its members to reflect on how they can be better stewards of all that God has entrusted to them.

The first principle, that all we have comes from God and he has entrusted us as stewards to look after his wealth, forms the basis for the other principles.

The second principle is that we need to be active in our care, or stewardship, of the resources with which God has provided us. While we must avoid the love of money, we should not neglect it either. Making effective use of our resources will require time and attention. It is incredibly easy to spend money, but making sure we do so wisely can be far harder. Attached to this book is a card you can put in your wallet or purse to remind you of these principles when you are making spending decisions.

The third principle, that we should seek to live within our resources, addresses the lifestyle implications of spending, credit and debt. If we can make decisions based on these principles to ensure that our income is greater than our costs of living, then we can generate resources for furthering God's mission in the world.

In this way we can build treasure in heaven, rather than on earth, which is the fourth principle. Jesus taught that our heart and our treasure are likely to be in the same place. Building treasure in heaven doesn't mean that Christians shouldn't save or contribute to pension funds. And we will explore issues such as saving, pensions and insurance as well as how we can support God's work.

The final principle suggests that we should be generous in our giving – of our time, of ourselves, of our homes and of our money. In giving to others we have the opportunity to reflect something of God's nature. Why? Because our God is a giving God, and has given generously to us. In our giving we reflect his life, and his love is extended – whether directly as we show hospitality or care, or indirectly through resourcing others to carry out God's work through the local church or other organizations.

We will look at what the Bible has to say about each of these principles, but since there are over 2,300 verses in the Bible on money, wealth and possessions, a short book such as this cannot provide an exhaustive view of Christian approaches to handling our money. But since God talks so much about the subject, it is important for us to begin to come to grips with it. If this book helps you move along in a process of reflection and exploration, it will have fulfilled its aim.

Why a Money 'Revolution'?

The dictionary offers a number of definitions for 'revolution'. Let's look at two of them.

a. A movement in, or as if in, a circle, or a complete turn in such a circle.

Here is the first sense of a money revolution – we recycle and return, as a gift, that which God has generously given us. As King David said, 'Everything comes from you, and we have given you only what comes from your hand' (1 Chron. 29:14), a phrase we frequently use in offertory prayers.

b. A far-reaching and drastic change, especially in ideas, methods etc.

What we will see throughout this book is that biblical teaching on money is a much-needed counter to the consumer's live-for-the-moment view of life. True riches are not those piled up in property, bank accounts or possessions but rather treasure in heaven, accumulated by giving of ourselves, of our time and of our money. The final chapter estimates the scale of the difference Christians could make to our world if such principles were widely adopted.

This book is intended as a workbook. If you live with a partner, it may be helpful to complete the worksheets in this book together. Alternatively, a trusted friend can provide encouragement and challenge as you work through this material. The worksheets will enable you to discover quite quickly and easily how the five principles apply to you and your situation. If you prefer to do this electronically, you can download an Excel spreadsheet from the web at www.themoneyrevolution.net.

Working through these principles is likely to have a direct impact on your life and finances. Those who live by these principles tend to find that they have less debt and are able to reduce their household outgoings by several hundred pounds a year or more. Not only that, you may also feel that you are more in control of your money, and that you can discover more of the joy that comes from giving to resource God's work and storing up 'treasure in heaven'.

There are a range of other resources provided on the web at www.themoneyrevolution.net:

■ Spreadsheets to help you reflect on your finances.

- Topical comments and news to help you to continue to apply these principles.

- A PowerPoint presentation and notes to allow you to share 'The Money Revolution' principles with others.

- A range of sermon notes to help church leaders preach effectively about the relationship between faith and money. Many churches only talk about money reluctantly, as and when the church's financial situation requires attention.

- Discussion guides for five home group sessions, one on each of the five principles.

PRINCIPLE 1
Everything Belongs to God

The first of the Money Revolution's five principles is that everything belongs to God – the land and natural creation, ourselves, and also our money and possessions – and we are stewards taking care of all that God has provided for us.

This principle requires us to accept three things, which we shall explore one at a time:

PRINCIPLE 1: Everything belongs to God.

1. God is the ultimate owner of all things.

2. God chooses to entrust the care, or stewardship, of many different resources to us.

3. We are accountable for how we care for these resources.

God is the ultimate owner of all things

A consumerist society emphasizes ownership – we buy, we own, we enjoy. Things that we have bought are at our own pleasure and disposal. God's ultimate ownership of everything is a revolutionary concept in a materialistic world. However, Jews and Christians should not find it revolutionary, for the Old Testament establishes this principle clearly. For example, we read verses such as the following in the Psalms:

> The earth is the LORD's, and everything in it, the world, and all who live in it. (Ps. 24:1)

> The heavens are yours, and yours also the earth; you founded the world and all that is in it. (Ps. 89:11)

King David understood this principle well. In 1 Chronicles 29 we read his prayer after the Israelites had donated materials to build the temple. As the materials were gathered, David prayed, 'But who am I, and who are my people, that we should be able to give as generously as this? Everything comes from you, and we have given you only what comes from your hand' (v. 14). David recognized that all riches and possessions come as a result of God's blessing.

Yes, our money belongs to God; yes, our house and land, and our possessions, belong to God; but, most significant of all, we ourselves belong to God.

> LORD, I know that people's lives are not their own; it is not for them to direct their steps. (Jer. 10:23)

> For we do not live to ourselves alone and we do not die to ourselves alone. If we live, we live to the Lord; and if we die, we die to the Lord. So, whether we live or die, we belong to the Lord. (Rom. 14:7, 8)

God entrusts us with stewardship responsibility

Part of understanding that God is the owner of everything is recognizing that the nature of God's ownership is fundamentally different to that which we often see modelled by human owners. Rather than a jealous, protective, 'it's mine' attitude, in God's ownership we see a generous sharing that grants us the freedom to act as we think fit.

Jesus told a parable of a man going on a journey who entrusted his property and wealth to his servants (Matt. 25:14–30). This man entrusted three servants with different amounts of money, and he gave each one the freedom to exercise stewardship over it. Each of the servants responded to this responsibility in a different way.

The word 'stewardship' is often misunderstood. It simply describes the responsibility of looking after something entrusted to another, while the owner retains his or her ownership. Suppose, for example, you ask someone to house-sit while you take an overseas holiday. During that time the housesitter, as a steward of the house, is empowered to make decisions to look after the property. If a water pipe bursts, the housesitter will take the appropriate action to repair and care for your property. During the time housesitters assume these responsibilities, they also have the privilege of enjoying the house and the benefits of living there.

This stewardship responsibility goes right back to the accounts of creation. In Genesis 1:28 and 2:15, we read about God giving humankind the responsibility to work the earth and to care for it. Our stewardship responsibility of caring for the planet is a crucial issue, and because of our understanding of God's creation Christians should contribute vigorously to the environmental debate.

We are accountable

The third point arising from the challenge of being stewards is that we are accountable to God for the way we handle his resources. As Paul says, 'Now it is required that those who have been given a trust must prove faithful' (1 Cor. 4:2). Just as in the parable of the talents the master returned to see the results of the stewardship each of the servants had exercised, so God will also hold us to account for our stewardship of the resources with which we have been entrusted. This is indeed a serious responsibility. It surely challenges us to take decisions not according to what we think is best for ourselves, but rather to seek to understand the wishes of the ultimate owner of our resources. And perhaps the most challenging and telling area of our stewardship responsibility is in the area of money.

The traditional covenant prayer Methodists use to renew their commitment at the start of a New Year reflects this responsibility. It begins, 'I am no longer my own, but yours', and continues, 'I freely and heartily yield all things to thy pleasure and disposal.' This prayer not only recognizes God's ownership, but also acknowledges our position as stewards who freely and heartily subject themselves to the Master. This is indeed challenging.

The Bible makes it clear that everything – all the earth, everyone in it, all their possessions and all their money – belongs to God. God has graciously entrusted his money to us and expects us to be wise and diligent in how we handle his money. He asks us to co-operate with him in using money to further his purposes on the earth. Consequently, just as members of the early church held no claims of ownership on their money or possessions, neither should we – since ultimately they belong to God.

Application **Count Your Blessings**

In this chapter we pause to reflect on the implications of this first principle as we consider just how richly God has blessed us in all sorts of ways.

The word we use to describe God's giving is 'grace', a word which conveys God's overflowing generosity, in spite of the fact that we do not merit such blessing. Indeed, it is grace precisely because we do not deserve it.

There is nothing we can do to earn grace – we can never be good enough to deserve the abundance of God's generosity. Archbishop Rowan Williams once described it thus: 'receiving the grace of God is like a crevice halfway down the Niagara Falls saying that it receives some water! Receiving isn't the word to describe the abundance of the water.' Grace is an integral part of God's character, and our only response to that grace can be to receive it.

God's giving is not only abundant; it is sacrificial. No one can give more than themselves, and in Jesus' death on the cross God gives of himself. In redeeming us through the death of Jesus, God has given everything possible.

While it is true that it is 'more blessed to give than to receive' (Acts 20:35), we need to learn to receive as well as to give. Our receiving should express thankfulness and joy and, in order to do that, we need to recognize all that we have been given. Sometimes we can take it for granted.

We begin by counting our financial blessings – not because they are more important, but because this is a book on Christian principles for managing money. Then we follow with a broader reflection on other blessings we have received.

What You Own, What You Owe

Assets (what you own)	Value	Value	Total Value
House(s) (if owned)			
Contents			
Bank Account(s)			
Savings Account(s)			
Stocks, Shares, ISAs			
Other Assets (car(s), antiques, jewellery, boat, caravan etc)			
Total Assets			

Liabilities (what you owe)	Value	Value	Total Value
Mortgage(s)			
Car Loans			
Other Short-term Loans			
Credit Card Balance Carried forward			
Total Liabilities			
Assets – Liabilities = Net Financial Worth			

God has not just blessed most of us financially. We have all received blessings from God in numerous other areas. God's creation, which we can all enjoy, is a gift. All of us have many things for which we thank God.

Pause for a few minutes here to reflect and list some of God's gifts for which you can give thanks. Some of us will name families, friends or loved ones; some enjoy good health; others are grateful for fulfilling work, leisure pursuits, opportunities to serve, or freedom from worry about basic needs such as food, clothing and safety.

Four things I am thankful for:

1.

2.

3.

4.

Some of the things that come to mind are blessings that are simply there for us to enjoy; our loving God has given us good things. In other areas, such as our money, our gifts and talents, and our time, we will need to exercise stewardship as we seek to use these things for God.

 Spend a moment in prayer, thanking God for his provision for you and for the blessings that you have received, and asking God for wisdom in your stewardship. Imagine the power of the water of Niagara reflected in God's generosity to you, and remember the nature of grace – his generous giving is not because of what you've done, or because you've earned it, but because of God's love for you.

You might like to use the following prayer:

Loving Lord, thank you for your generosity to me. May I realize afresh each day how gracious and generous you are. Help me to be a good steward of all that you have entrusted to me. As I exercise that stewardship, help me to reflect your generosity to the world around me. Amen.

PRINCIPLE 2
Active Stewardship

The second principle of the Money Revolution asserts that we all need to be active stewards of the resources that God is entrusting to our care. The idea of financial planning or budgeting does not appeal to most of us. If we don't have to, then why should we? Often those of us who make a budget do so because money is tight. Many people see getting to a point where they no longer have to budget as a sign of financial success.

> **PRINCIPLE 2:**
> **Be active in your stewardship.**

Yet planning your spending is the only way you can make sure that you are controlling your money and exercising choice about how it is used. Money tends to leak – largely as a result of successful marketing, which creates desires we never thought we had and attracts us with products which promise to satisfy those newly created desires. In the book of Haggai, God describes the bottomless pit of greed and careless stewardship as putting money 'in a purse with holes in it'. By contrast, God reminds his people then – and now – to 'give careful thought to your ways' (Hag. 1:5,6).

We tend to find that as our income rises, so does our level of spending. As many people get wealthier throughout their lives, so their desires seem to increase in proportion. We want the more expensive car, the larger house, branded clothes, gadgets and foreign holidays. Our view of what constitutes 'a luxury' changes as we have more disposable income. Often we aren't making these decisions consciously, but because of this tendency it is all the more important that we budget. According to the analogy in Haggai, the more we have, the bigger the holes in our purses seem to be.

One of the challenges we face is balancing our long-term priorities with short-term choices. In exchanging the inheritance of his birthright for a bowl of Jacob's red lentil stew, Esau provides an example of the compelling nature of short-term desire (Gen. 25). Budgeting effectively helps us to take an overview of both long-term and short-term priorities, and to balance them appropriately.

There are four steps in setting and using a budget:

1. *Identify* how much money you have coming in.

2. *Evaluate* where the money is currently spent.

3. *Review* current spending patterns and identify changes
   you wish to make.

4. *Track* this over time to make sure that you are achieving
   the aims set in step 3.

In this chapter we will look at the first two steps. We will explore step 3 in the action planning chapter at the end of the book, which will encourage you to set a date to carry out step 4.

Paul urges us to avoid the love of money and reminds us not to focus on it too much. Careful management of money is good, yet we should not give it too much attention. So it is important to strike a healthy balance – we need to manage our finances wisely without becoming obsessed with them.

With good budgeting we can identify areas of priority action and focus on these.

Step 1: Identifying income

This stage is important, because you may find that you have more income than you realized. As you work through this chapter, you will find it helpful to have bank statements, bills and other personal finance information to hand.

When completing the table below, you should include all regular income, even if it requires dividing regular annual income by 12. But exclude all one-off income (e.g., legacies, windfalls etc.). Many bills are paid monthly, so the tool is based on monthly income and expenditure. However, if you have weekly income or bills, you should multiply up to express them as monthly equivalents.

Budget Planner

Regular Monthly Income	£ per Month
Wage 1: Monthly take-home pay	
Wage 2: Monthly take-home pay	
Pension Income	
Benefits	
Income from Savings	
Income from Shares, Trusts, etc.	
Other Income	
Total regular Monthly Income	

Step 2: Evaluating where the money is being spent

For this step, enter all of your monthly outgoings into the table that follows.

You may be surprised to see that charitable giving is listed as the first line. The reason for this will become clear when we discuss our fifth principle.

In reviewing your spending, you will need to calculate an 'average month', adding up bills for a year and dividing by 12. To work out your insurance costs, you may find the worksheet on page 44 helpful. If your review shows that a large amount of your spending is in cash, you might need to make a note of where you spend this money for a week or two to gauge where the money is actually going.

 The two final stages of this budgeting process, where you consider whether your budget reflects your priorities, are presented in the final chapter. However, you might like to pause at this point for thought and prayerful reflection. What does the above exercise reveal to you about your financial priorities as they stand today?

Monthly Expenses

Charitable Giving
Church	Other Regular Giving		Estimated Spontaneous Giving	Total

Housing
Mortgage/Rent	Council Tax	Maintenance	Other	

Utilities
Electricity	Gas/Oil	Water/Sewerage	Telecoms	

Food and Household
Groceries	All Eating Out	Household Needs	Clothes	

Leisure (inc monthly subscriptions)	Holidays	Electricals	Other	

Transport
Bus/Train Fares	Petrol/Parking	MOT/Car Tax	Repairs & Tyres	

Insurance
Take figure from p.44

Savings and Investments — All regular savings contributions

Loan Repayments — All unsecured loan repayments

Credit/Debit Card Payments — Average all other payments

Total Monthly Expenses

Finally, calculate the gap between income and expenditure:

Total Income — Total Expenditure = Surplus/Deficit

PRINCIPLE 3
Live within Your Resources

The third principle of the Money Revolution is that we need to live within our resources. If we can create a gap between our regular income and our regular expenditure, we have the opportunity to save, to give or to treat ourselves to something special. On the other hand, however, if our expenditure is greater than our income, and we are sliding steadily into greater and greater debt, then not only do we not have opportunities to give or to save, but it becomes increasingly harder to pay off the mounting debt.

PRINCIPLE 3:
Live within your
resources.

Recent statistics on UK debt show that: we are, on average, taking out significant levels of unsecured debt; we have the highest ever levels of mortgage borrowing; and the number of individual bankruptcies and voluntary agreements (IVAs) is at its highest ever level. Total UK personal debt exceeds £1,000 billion, and average household debt excluding mortgages is over £8,000. The average household pays over £3,000 debt interest each year (including mortgage interest).

While this chapter focuses on credit and debt, those who are not in debt should not skip it. The prevalence of debt is such that those who have successfully avoided high personal debt may be called upon to advise those struggling with debt. Some of the thoughts offered in this chapter may also be helpful to those without significant debt.

Credit and debt

Most people in the UK will find themselves in debt at one time or another, for all sorts of reasons. Purchasing a house is likely to require us to take on a mortgage, and choosing to study at university will lead most students to take out student loans. Both of these are long-term debts. There are many other situations which can lead to short-term debt, such as illness, losing a job, having a baby or a change in family situation. All of these can make it difficult to manage a household budget.

Others choose to take on additional loans in order to acquire a better car, a new sofa or TV, or take a more expensive holiday. Advertising and promotions encourage us to buy these things before we have the cash to do so. Loans are very easy to come by, and advertised low rates of interest, or loans that are interest free, can disguise the fact that we are still taking on additional debt.

As a result, many people have several different loans which need to be repaid. At the same time, they continue to incur regular household expenses and need to keep up with the rent or mortgage, provide for a family and so on. In this chapter we will look at some of the factors involved in taking on debt; reflect on Christian principles regarding debt; and, finally, we will explore ways of getting out of debt.

Debt and debtors in the Bible

There are several verses in the Bible which help us consider debt and how we should live. One such oft-quoted verse is Romans 13:8: 'Let no debt remain outstanding, except the continuing debt to love one another, for whoever loves others has fulfilled the law.' In the context of the surrounding verses (vv. 1–10), Paul appears to have a wider agenda than simply money, but he also considers taxes, respect and honour. The principle here is that we must fulfil our obligations – except the continuing debt to love one another, which we can never fully discharge.

Matthew 5:42 records Jesus saying, 'do not turn away from the one who wants to borrow from you'. On several other occasions, Jesus referred to the subject of debt in his teaching: in the parable of the unmerciful servant (Matt. 18:23–35); in answering the question about which servant loved their master more (Lk. 7:41–43); and in the parable of the shrewd manager (Lk. 16:1–9). In none of these parables is the debt itself seen as sinful or evil, although the debtor who would not show mercy, after receiving much greater mercy, is condemned. But the condemnation is on account of his lack of mercy, rather than because he was either a debtor or a lender. Borrowing and debt were clearly a routine part of life in first-century Palestine, and Jesus does not expressly forbid it.

So debt is not in itself a sin, but the Bible does speak against charging 'exorbitant interest' (Prov. 28:8); forbids making a profit from the poor, or lending them money at interest (Lev. 25:35–38); and encourages us to be content with what we have (1 Tim. 6:6–10). It is building up debt in order to chase the dreams of consumerism, and the love of money and its spending power, that Paul writes of as being the root of evil (1 Tim. 6:10).

While debt is not wrong, it is undesirable. Proverbs says that 'the rich rule over the poor, and the borrower is slave to the lender' (Prov. 22:7). Again, lending and borrowing are not sinful, just as it is not a sin to be poor or rich. Rather, this proverb reveals the changed nature of relationships once one enters into debt.

Our third principle, therefore, is that as Christians we seek to live within the resources with which God has provided us. In some situations entering into an element of debt is a necessary part of our culture. This can be compatible with this third principle as long as we are handling money wisely, the interest charged is minimised and paying off the debt is manageable within our income.

Taking on debt

As we have seen, debt is not always wrong. Debt can be most dangerous when we incur it as a result of living above our means, or when the debt that we have taken on is an unwise form of financing. Some forms of debt are part of twenty-first century life in Britain and raise some particular questions. Here we address four of these questions, regarding mortgages, credit cards, student loans and interest-free offers.

 DO MORTGAGES COUNT AS DEBT?

The simple answer is that mortgages are indeed debts – and those debts will need to be repaid at some point in the future. However, because of their link with the provision of housing, as well as the fact that they are secured by an asset, mortgages are a very different kind of debt to that created by excess spending on a credit card.

There are perhaps two things to consider regarding mortgages:

1. First, is the mortgage affordable? If you took it on would you still be able to live within your means? Mortgage companies assess affordability in terms of lending a multiple of the salaries of the applicants. In recent years the available multiple has increased, and lenders will now offer up to five times the applicant's salary. However, just because a lender is prepared to lend a certain amount of money doesn't mean that it is a wise debt to take

on. What is affordable now may not be affordable in the future if interest rates were to rise, and this should be considered.

2. Second, the mortgage being considered should be compared with the value of the property – the 'loan to value' rate. Predicting future house prices is impossible, and it would be prudent to allow for a buffer between the mortgage and the house's current value, in case you had to sell during a market correction.

WHAT ABOUT STUDENT LOANS?

It seems impossible to get through university without taking on loans. There are many who decry a government policy that requires young people to take on significant levels of debt in order to extend their education. The prospect of such debt, however, should not prevent someone from entering higher education. The interest charged on approved student loan schemes is limited to a measure of inflation, and the loan is only required to be repaid after qualification, once incomes are above a certain threshold.

The key challenges for students are to minimize the debt that they leave college with, and also to ensure that any debt is kept as far as possible to approved student loan schemes. Running up large overdrafts and credit card debts can be a hugely expensive way of financing education and can create significant financial problems in the years immediately after graduation as overdrafts and credit card loans will need to be paid off irrespective of earnings.

HOW SHOULD WE USE A CREDIT CARD?

While it is possible to live in twenty-first century Britain without some form of plastic card, it is increasingly difficult since shopping online, by telephone or mail order often cannot be done without card details. Debit cards are probably preferable, since they reduce the temptation to spend above your means. However, if you are able to control your spending and pay them off by monthly direct debit, credit cards can be effective in certain situations (e.g., for charging refundable expenses, since this allows time to receive the money back before having to settle the bills). If using a credit card affects whether or not you buy something, then you might ask whether it is wise for you to make the purchase.

DO INTEREST-FREE OFFERS COUNT AS DEBT?

This question often arises because interest-free offers – credit agreements or debts – carry no financial penalty for paying later. The best way to benefit from such an offer is to move the funds into a savings account so that you accrue some interest before you pay off the debt. If, however, you cannot afford the item at the time of purchase, can you be sure you will be able to meet the payments?

Taking action over debt

It is a good idea to review your debt levels at regular intervals. It is healthy to be in a position where your level of debt is reducing, rather than increasing.

Reducing your debt can also have a positive impact for God's work. Rather than repaying interest to the bank or credit card company, money can be used to fund mission work, to combat poverty, or to further other charitable work.

Here are six steps to enable you to take action over your debt.

1. Complete a thorough review

The worksheet on the next page is a useful tool to help you reflect on your total debt situation. The important thing is to consider these debts in the light of your monthly income and expenses (see pages 20 and 21).

Compare your levels of debt from this table with your levels of income. Consider whether you need to take action. For lower levels of debt, you may be able to bring your finances back into shape by following the next five points. If, however, your debt feels significant, is causing you anxiety, or you are struggling to pay off more than the minimum repayments on credit card bills, you are encouraged to seek expert advice, which is available free. See the end of this chapter for a list of places where such advice is freely available.

Debts Review

Owed to:	Amount Outstanding
Overdraft	
Credit Cards	
Store Cards	
Other Unsecured Loans (Car, General, etc.)	
Hire-Purchase Agreements	
Arrears on Rent, Mortgage or other Loans	
Total Owing	

2. Increase your income

Your ability to reduce debt depends on how much of a gap you can create between the money you have coming in and going out each month. In the short term, spending more than you earn may lead you into levels of debt you consider manageable but, left unchecked over the longer term, this kind of spending can cause significant problems.

Consider whether you can increase your income in the short term to reduce your debt levels. Are there opportunities to earn overtime or to take on additional work?

3. Reduce your spending

Reducing your spending is more significant than increasing your income. Assuming you are a taxpayer, at least one fifth of every extra pound you earn will go to the government in income tax. You are also likely to incur some incremental costs when you earn additional money (e.g., travelling costs).

Most people begin a spending review with the idea that there is little they will be able to do to reduce costs. But every single pound saved is a pound that can be used to repay debts. The rest of this chapter and the next chapter, on good spending, include guidelines that will be helpful.

You may, however, benefit from taking some more significant action in the short term.

- Check your monthly direct debits – satellite TV, health club, phone extras, etc. Do you really need them? Stopping them will make a saving month in, month out – not just once.

- What do you spend on leisure: cinema, eating out, trips? Don't just guess – add it up for the last three months. Could you commit to reduce this for the next few months?

- What about holidays? Could you stay at home this year and take short trips in your local area? What other free or cheap holiday options do you have?

- Could you use the car less?

While these are quite drastic action steps, you will need to take significant action if you have significant debt. They may not be easy steps, but they may be necessary ones for a while so you can get your finances back into good shape.

If you are going to buy something, try to use hard cash instead of a credit, store or debit card. If you count out the notes, it will probably feel like you are paying more than when you simply hand over a piece of plastic. It may also help you manage your cash flow better to avoid incurring unnecessary interest.

4. Prioritize your debts

The interest you pay on your debt is probably the greatest waste of your money. So our first aim should always be to try not to incur any additional debt. Also make sure that you pay off mortgage or rent arrears – if they are not under control you could lose your home.

The worst form of credit is that which has a high annualized percentage rate of interest (APR); the higher the APR, the more you will be paying back in interest, and the original amount borrowed can easily spiral into huge insurmountable debts. Store cards generally have the highest APR – as high as 33%. Usually credit cards or hire purchase have the next highest APR, followed by bank loans or unauthorized overdrafts. If you default on any monthly repayments on these products you will probably incur an extra charge, which makes the loan even more expensive.

Paying off your loan with the highest APR first will have the greatest impact on reducing the amount you will have to repay. Usually bank loans cannot be repaid early, but discuss your options with the bank manager and look out for penalty clauses for an early settlement in any of your contracts.

Consider cutting up your credit or store cards, as this will remove temptation to incur further debt.

Zero interest and consolidation

Many companies have introductory offers which allow you to transfer your existing credit card debt onto the new credit card, often for an interest-free period, or with a very low interest rate for the first few months. While this is worth looking into, as with all things be sure to read the small print and ask for the relevant information to be put in writing. Never sign anything unless you are absolutely sure you know all the pros and cons. By choosing carefully you could save hundreds of pounds. Remember that these offers are made not to help consumers, but to entice them into a relationship which will be profitable in the longer term to the credit card company.

You may wish to consider consolidating your debts by taking out a loan with a lower APR to cover them all. While a lower APR will make it easier to pay off your debt more quickly, if the consolidated loan is secured against your house this may not be the best option.

Never fall for the temptation of taking out a slightly larger loan than you need to pay off your existing debts, so that you can have a good holiday or treat yourself. The bottom line is this: make sure that you are paying the lowest possible interest on the smallest possible debt.

5. Put aside some emergency savings

In good times, it's a sound move to plan for harsher times. Even in difficult times, it's a good idea to try to save something. Even a small fund for emergencies can make a significant difference.

Why? Imagine your washing machine stops working and you have no money at all. What do you do? Many people would resort, perhaps reluctantly, to using their credit card to purchase a new one – feeling justified that they had to increase their debt for this. Because it's being added to the debt, you may feel freer to buy something more expensive. This increases your debt, as does the additional interest the credit card will incur.

But if you had £200 in an emergency fund you would have a couple of other options – maybe you could get the old one repaired. Or you might find a good used one which had been checked for safety and had a guarantee, quite possibly from a shop which doesn't take credit cards in order to keep its prices low.

6. Consider if you need to take further action

If you feel that your debts are more significant than you can handle, you should seek professional advice immediately. There are several alternatives to consider, and such advisers can help you think through the options. You don't have to pay for this kind of advice – there are several free services which can help you.

For free debt advice in the UK contact:

- Consumer Credit Counselling Service (CCCS): 0800 138 1111
- Online debt advice at www.creditaction.org.uk
- Payplan: 0800 389 3431
- Money Advice Scotland (www.moneyadvicescotland.org.uk)
- Citizens Advice (www.cas.org.uk)

Application **Good Spending**

Trying to spend according to Christian principles is one of the most difficult challenges many Christians face. Why? Purchasing decisions are complex, with a number of factors to sift through, and we are making these decisions all the time.

These decisions range from choices in the supermarket regarding what breakfast cereals to buy to major purchases like cars and houses. Every purchase decision we make reveals something about our priorities and principles.

While individually we may feel that we are powerless, caught up in a society where we cannot make a difference, together Christians can make their influence felt. If you assume that, on average, the income of Christian households is in line with the national average, then each year the spending of Christian households amounts to a total of £56 billion. This is a staggeringly large amount of money, and it can influence manufacturers and retailers.

The wider stocking of Fair Trade products is a good example of a change initiated by Christians and others with a concern for exploited workers. These advances have resulted not only from disciplined purchasing – people spending their money in line with their principles – but also from lobbying retailers to provide such goods.

We are constantly bombarded with messages trying to persuade us to purchase on impulse, rather than in a principled or considered way. As we watch TV, read magazines or walk around the supermarket, the aim of advertising and marketing is to encourage us to make a sudden decision to spend money on something that catches our eye. In the face of this it's important to be disciplined, and to maintain the self-control which is a fruit of the Holy Spirit's work in our lives. 'Like a city whose walls are broken through is a person who lacks self-control' (Prov. 25:28). This doesn't mean we should never purchase things that catch our eye. It is a wonderful blessing to be able to afford some discretionary purchases, to buy things that we want and don't necessarily need.

Knowing the difference between our wants and our needs is vital, and wisdom is crucial when making spending decisions. The six pointers below will help you reflect on spending decisions, particularly significant ones. Most of us would admit that we make poor purchases from time to time. If we can reduce these, we will be better stewards of our resources, able to free more funds to use for saving or for supporting God's work.

Six pointers to a good purchase decision

1. Good spending is consistent with our values. The best spending decisions will not always result in us buying the cheapest products. There are many factors to consider. Does a £3 pair of jeans allow a decent wage for those involved in the manufacture of the product? How important to you are organic, free-range and other food production issues? What significance do you place on buying recycled or recyclable products? What environmental considerations does the purchase of a product raise – including, for example, flying fruit halfway around the world. The ways that we spend our money can give testimony to our Christian values, and can have just as great an impact as our giving.

2. Are you going to use it? A fantastic offer is really a very poor deal unless you are going to use it. Stores are full of signs proclaiming 'save 20%', '33% off' or even 'save 50%', yet we can save 100% if we don't buy the item. If we buy a £250 camera reduced to £150, we don't save £100, we spend £150. We have £150 less at our disposal.

Every year Britons spend over £2 billion purchasing gadgets for the home, many of which are seldom used. Sandwich toasters, bedside tea and coffee machines, bread-makers, fitness machines, electric DIY tools and so on. If they are well used, then they can represent excellent value – giving us fresh bread, saving on calling out tradesmen and keeping us healthy. However, I suspect most of us can think of a purchase, probably bought on impulse in a sale, for which, even with the price reduction, the cost per use is staggeringly high because we simply haven't used it.

A recent survey on food in Britain suggests that up to 30% of all that we produce and manufacture is wasted, at a cost of between £8 billion and £16 billion a year. This has profound waste implications, as well as a financial impact. Around 17 million tonnes of food are taken to landfill sites each year.

3. Consider the long-term cost, not just the purchase price. For example, buying a tent or caravan can lead to all sorts of additional costs on top of the initial purchase: awning, camping equipment and accessories, as well as pitch fees. Camping and caravanning can still offer good value compared to other forms of holidays – but the point is that the cost can be greater than it first appears.

Our family was given two rabbits a couple of years ago. A free gift ended up costing hundreds of pounds after the cage, run, food and bedding had been bought, not to mention significant vet bills when they fell ill. Calculate the expected long-term cost before you buy – many things will work out to be much more expensive than they seem at first.

4. Spend an appropriate amount of time shopping around. The greater the cost, the more worthwhile it is to shop around. The internet and telephone allow you to compare prices without having to spend time in lots of different shops. As we've seen, buying the cheapest product on offer isn't necessarily the smartest buy – either because of poorer quality or because of concerns over the ethical employment policies of the manufacturer.

5. Pray about major purchases. Committing to buy a major item is a significant decision. Money spent on one item is no longer available for other purposes. Just as we should pray about other significant decisions in our lives such as jobs or where we choose to live, we can pray for wisdom in making large spending decisions.

6. Does it have to be new? Buying some items second-hand can give very good value. A one-year-old car is thousands of pounds cheaper than it was when it was new. Buying a book from a second-hand bookshop can save pounds, compared to the cost of buying new. And borrowing a book from a library is free. Sometimes it doesn't make sense to buy second-hand. A used child's car-seat, for example, would probably not be a wise buy, as there is no way to test if it still meets safety standards. Consider selling, as well as buying, second-hand. Taking a few boxes of items you've finished with down to a car boot sale can make some money and be fun.

These six pointers are on the back of the card fixed to the front of this book. Placing this in your wallet will remind you of these factors when you are making a significant decision.

Good spending is linked with green spending

As we saw above, good stewardship is not just about buying the cheapest products possible. In our stewardship of the planet, sometimes we will need to make a small investment up front. Yet, very often, choosing a greener option saves money in the long run.

Here are 10 tips to help you be environmentally responsible.

 Ten tips for good stewardship of our finances and the planet

1. **Lighting**. Replacing an ordinary light bulb with an energy saving bulb could save £9 a year by converting less electricity into heat, and these bulbs last up to 12 times longer.

2. **Turning off**. Cut your electricity bills up to 10% by turning electrical products off, rather than leaving them on standby.

3. **Increase driving economy**. Driving smoothly; changing gear at lower revs and keeping your speed down can increase fuel economy significantly.

4. **Insulation**. Rolls of loft insulation are not expensive, and a 270-millimetre (approx. 10.5 inches) layer could save around £200 a year on fuel bills.

5. **Heating**. Every degree centigrade that you turn a room thermostat down by can save up to £30 a year.

6. **Walk or cycle for short journeys**. Many car journeys are shorter than a mile. Consider walking or biking – you'll use less fuel and get some healthy exercise.

7. **Collect rainwater for your garden**. Butts and diverters to collect from downpipes can be purchased from most DIY stores.

8. **Measure your consumption**. Check how much power an appliance is using with a plug-in meter, or measure the total energy consumption of your home to find where energy is leaking. You could share a meter between friends or within the church.

9. **Hot water**. Make sure that the insulating jacket around your hot water tank is at least 75 millimetres (or 3 inches) thick. You could save around £20 per year.

10. **Print again**. Over 40 million printer cartridges go into UK landfill sites each year. Consider buying refilled cartridges instead.

With a little creativity and thought, you will find numerous opportunities in your everyday life and work to conserve and save. More ideas and links at www.themoneyrevolution.net.

PRINCIPLE 4
Build up Treasure in Heaven

The fourth principle of the Money Revolution is based on Matthew 6, where Jesus teaches 'Do not store up for yourselves treasures on earth, where moth and rust destroy, and where thieves break in and steal. But store up for yourselves treasures in heaven, where moth and rust do not destroy, and where thieves do not break in and steal' (Matt. 6:19–22).

Why not treasure on earth?

Jesus taught about the futility of pursuing treasure on earth, but even then it was nothing new. In the Old Testament, the fifth chapter of Ecclesiastes contains some verses about money which are as relevant today as they were two and half thousand years ago: 'Those who love money never have enough; those who love wealth are never satisfied with their income' (v. 10).

> **PRINCIPLE 4:**
> Build up treasure
> in heaven, not on
> earth.

Regardless of how much money we have, we don't have enough. At every level of wealth, human ambition aspires for a little more, yearning for that which is always just out of reach. John D. Rockefeller once said, 'I have made many millions, but they have brought me no happiness'. Many lottery winners, whose dreams of lifelong joy and happiness are left unfilled, have echoed this sentiment.

'As goods increase, so do those who consume them. And what benefit are they to the owners except to feast their eyes on them?' (v. 11). This passage emphasizes the waste of excess – that when our needs have been satisfied, and we move on to seeking to fulfil wants and luxuries, then we often achieve little, except for the dubious pleasure of gazing at our possessions.

Indeed, the more we have, the more we have to worry about. 'The sleep of labourers is sweet, whether they eat little or much, but the abundance of the rich permits them no sleep' (v. 12).

'Everyone comes naked from their mother's womb, and as everyone comes, so they depart. They take nothing from their toil that they can carry in their hands' (v. 15). This section ends with the timeless truth that everything that we store up in this life is left behind when we die.

The parable of the rich farmer (Lk. 12:16–21) echoes this teaching. The farmer builds up excess, always looking to some point in the future. That day never arrives, due to his untimely death, and his earthly treasure goes to waste in newly built barns.

Treasure and security

The parable of the rich farmer challenges us to examine where we place our hope and security. The farmer believed that a store of wealth would provide an easier future and security in the face of unanticipated rainy days. Yet in the face of death, the farmer's security was worthless. We too must face the question: where do we find security?

Saving, like insurance, does provide an element of protection against unpredictable events in the future. But sometimes we go far beyond a prudent provision for the future. It's possible to find that we have based our sense of identity and self-worth on the things we own. We can begin to define ourselves by the brands and possessions we buy. Much of the fashion and branding we see in magazines or on TV have nothing to do with quality and everything to do with image. Slogans such as 'Because I'm worth it' (L'Oreal), 'Just do it' (Nike) and 'Reassuringly expensive' (Stella Artois) tell us nothing about the benefits of what we buy – they appeal to our desire to be different to how we are today.

Treasure and where our hearts are

As Jesus teaches about where we store up our treasure, he makes it clear that our priorities and our heart are inextricably linked.

We return to the episode of Jesus' encounter with a rich young man, recorded in Matthew 19, Mark 10 and Luke 18. It is helpful to note that in all three gospel accounts Jesus links giving to the poor with building up treasure in heaven as he challenges the man to give away his accumulated wealth.

Why? We don't have the capacity to have two number-one things in our life. 'No one can serve two masters . . . You cannot serve both God and Money' (Matt. 6:24). We have a choice. The Greek word *mamona* (Mammon) is the same in Aramaic, and its root meaning is that in which one has confidence. We cannot place our confidence, trust or loyalty in two places – if we did it would be divided loyalty. At its heart, the challenge of discipleship is single-minded commitment to follow Christ with all that we are, and all that we have.

Contentment

Contentment is the opposite of consumerism. A consumerist society seeks to make our possessions obsolete so we will replace them with new ones. New models of electrical goods are released every few months, with only minor changes to their functionality; changes in fashion render clothes out of date before they are worn out; and easy credit allows you to update your car or home furnishings just because you feel like a change. Paul, however, wrote to Timothy about being content with what we have. In 1 Timothy 6:1–10, Paul prefaces his well-known, but often misquoted, comment that 'the love of money is a root of all kinds of evil' with teaching on contentment.

Paul challenges those who think that godliness, or religion, is a means to financial gain. Rather, he suggests, 'godliness with contentment is great gain'. In other words, while the Bible teaches that those who are generous can expect to receive blessing, that blessing may not be financial prosperity but rather a peace of mind and contentment with what we have.

Paul continues, 'if we have food and clothing, we will be content with that'. He warns of the dangers of seeking riches: 'Those who want to get rich fall into temptation and a trap and into many foolish and harmful desires that plunge people into ruin and destruction.'

Seeking treasure on earth can lead us into all kinds of temptation, and placing too high a priority on it will divert us from placing our faith firmly in God's care for us. In Matthew 6 Jesus tells us not to worry about treasure on earth, for God knows our needs and will provide for them. Socrates was once asked, 'Who is the wealthiest man?' His answer? 'He who is content with the least.'

Where is your heart?

 Spend some time reflecting on where your priorities, and your heart, are. You might want to ask God to reveal to you areas where your heart and priorities are focused on building up treasure on earth, rather than in heaven.

Many of us will find that, at times, our hearts are not where we might like them to be. It is easy to get caught up with the financial worries of this world, or with material possessions. There are two practical things we can do to help bring our thoughts, our hearts and our treasure back in line.

Through completing the exercises and answering the questions posed throughout this book, we are already beginning to bring our thoughts, our hearts and our treasure back in line. We can also commit to building up treasure in heaven daily. We can make some larger decisions following a financial review, but we can also resolve to adopt a positive habit of making daily deposits.

How to make daily deposits

Just like accumulating savings on earth, the easiest way to build up treasure in heaven is by small, regular deposits. How? Jesus answered, 'If you want to be perfect, go, sell your possessions and give to the poor, and you will have treasure in heaven' (Matt. 19:21). Luke also records Jesus teaching that, as a result of trusting in God's provision, we should build up treasure in heaven by giving to the poor (Lk. 12:22–30).

Giving generously, whether of ourselves, our money, our time or our hospitality, needs to become a habit. Each day we might seek to do something that will be a practical expression of our generosity and, in so doing, we will build up our daily deposits of treasure in heaven.

Application **Take Cover?**

Television, mail, magazine advertising and the internet offer a huge variety of insurance. No longer are we restricted to insuring our houses, cars, life or health; we can take out insurance to extend a manufacturer's warranty on a kitchen appliance, to cover the health of pets or even to provide cover should the church fete be cancelled due to rain. Virtually any need can be insured.

What is a Christian view of insurance?

As in most areas of money and finance, we need to think through insurance carefully as there are a number of principles to draw together.

The first of these principles is to trust in God's future provision. In Matthew's Gospel, Jesus teaches us not to worry about what might happen in the future (Matt. 6:25–34). So if we trust God, do we need insurance? On the other hand, we might view insurance as a way of removing anxiety about the future. We are investing current resources in preparation for events that may affect us in the future.

The second principle is provision for our families. Paul wrote about the importance of making provision for immediate family members in his first letter to Timothy (1 Tim. 5:8). In twenty-first-century Britain, life insurance could be seen as an appropriate part of that provision.

Insurance is compulsory for some things, and the Bible teaches us to obey the law set down by civil authorities (Rom. 13:1–8). All car owners, for instance, are legally required to have a minimum level of cover. If a house is purchased with a mortgage, the mortgage company is likely to require that buildings insurance cover is taken out until the mortgage is paid off. If we are to live with integrity, then we need to carry out the conditions of the mortgage we have agreed to.

Since stewardship principles apply to our allocation of resources, we also need to consider them in our decisions about insurance cover. We need to remember that money is limited, and so when we decide to spend money in one area we will not have that money to spend on something else. For some areas of risk, it is prudent to take out protection against what would amount to a catastrophe. Other insurance policies may not be such good stewardship of our money, and therefore we need to think through our decisions policy by policy.

Getting good value

For the most commonly used areas of insurance, the market in the UK is very competitive, with brokers and the internet making it easy to compare quotations from different insurance companies. It is important to shop around. Insurance quotes are based on a calculation of the likelihood of the insurer having to pay out on a claim. Different insurers will calculate this risk differently, and this is why you can sometimes get wildly different quotes. The details of the cover offered may also vary, so do check the details to make sure you are getting the cover that best suits your needs.

The fact that the profit margins on house, car and life insurance policies are low would seem to indicate that people taking out these policies can get good value. However, one consequence of the competitive market for these types of insurance policies is that insurers seek to sell additional bolt-on policies that have much higher profit margins. Since, for example, the market for car insurance policies is competitive, quotes should offer good value. The basic quote, therefore, will probably be offered with a range of optional bolt-on policies covering breakdowns, legal expenses, claims management, and so on. For these additional policies, the underlying 'underwriting premium', or the part of the policy that goes to cover the risk itself, can be as low as 5%, or one twentieth, of the amount you pay.

It can be difficult to compare different products, and to assess whether you are getting good value. One example would be Payment Protection Insurance. In 2006, the Office of Fair Trading launched an investigation to explore issues relating to the availability of information for consumers choosing products, and the relatively high profit margins made by insurance companies on these kinds of products. This does not suggest that it is wrong to take out this kind of insurance, merely that we should take extra care to be certain that we are insuring the risks that we do not wish to carry, and that we are getting good value in doing so.

In the end, the value that insurance offers depends on whether the event that you are insuring against happens or not and how important it is to you to have peace of mind that you are covered should that eventuality occur. Life insurance is a great example – you hope the policy will not need to pay out, yet the peace of mind that comes from knowing that family and loved ones are protected is important to the policyholder. Calculating the amount of life insurance required is not easy. For life insurance for a primary breadwinner, for example, you may need to assume that loved ones will need an income from the insurance money, rather than simply spending the capital over time.

Self-insurance

In some areas, particularly where the insured event has a relatively low cost, an alternative is self-insurance. Rather than taking out an insurance policy, money is put aside into a savings account, to be used in the future should the risk become reality.

Extended warranties, or service agreements, which offer notoriously poor value, may be particularly suited to self-insurance.

Shops selling electrical items will often try to sell you an extended warranty at the point of sale, and salespeople are paid commission on the warranties they sell. Compared with the purchase price of the appliance, the price of extended warranties is significant, and the purchase decision should be thought through with as much care as the decision to buy the item in the first place. The frequency of breakdown, and the cost of repair, both affect the value of the extended warranty.

A recent Office of Fair Trading (OFT) investigation into extended warranties found that the average TV repair costs between £35 and £55. Thus if a four-year extended warranty on a £500 television cost £200, then the TV would need to break down four times in years two to five for you to be better off by taking out the extended warranty.

Conclusion

If you add up the total cost of all your insurance policies, you will probably find that you are spending more on insurance than you thought. For many households, this will be well into four figures. It is, therefore, worth pausing and considering your insurance needs carefully. The following action points may be helpful in doing this.

Action points

✓ Complete the checklist on the following page to ascertain how much you are spending each year on insurance.

✓ Review each policy to determine whether you need it, and whether it offers good value.

✓ Consider whether you will choose to self-insure some risks.

When you renew a policy:

✓ Do shop around to compare prices.

✓ Do read the policy details to make sure you are getting what you need.

✓ Think carefully about any additional items you may be offered.

Insurance checklist

You may be surprised by how much you spend on insurance in a given year. This checklist will help you assess your policies, and this information will help you to decide whether to maintain the policy as is, to shop around at the next annual renewal, to change the cover levels or to self-insure. Annual premiums should be entered, so if you pay monthly you will need to multiply your monthly premium by 12.

Insurance Checklist

Area of Insurance	Annual Premium	Action (Maintain, Shop Around, Change Cover or Self-insure)
HOME INSURANCE		
Buildings		
Contents		
Home Emergency		
LIFE AND HEALTH		
Life Insurance Policies		
Critical Illness Cover		
Medical		
Dental		
CARS		
Car 1		
Car 2		
Breakdown		
Additional Policies (e.g. Gap, MOT)		
OTHER AREAS		
Travel		
Pets		
Caravan/Boat		
Specialist Insurance		
Extended Warranty: Item 1		
Extended Warranty: Item 2		
TOTAL ANNUAL SPEND		

Application **Savings and Pensions**

Proverbs 6 enjoins us, 'Go to the ant, you sluggard; consider its ways and be wise! It has no commander, no overseer or ruler, yet it stores its provisions in summer and gathers its food at harvest' (vv. 6–8). This is wise advice. In the good times, if we are disciplined, we can build up a fund to help us in more difficult times in the future.

We will explore two principal issues regarding savings and pensions. First, how much should Christians save or invest? Second, what criteria should we apply in deciding where to save?

How much should we save?

There has been much written to guide Christian thinking on how much we should give, but very little advice about how much we should save.

In one sense, the answer is simple – when we look at the difference between our income and our spending, we can save that which we don't give. The fourth principle of building treasure in heaven rather than on earth challenges us regarding the split between what we save and what we give, and keeping this in mind may encourage us to give a little more and save a little less.

There are many different reasons to save – for an unforeseen need such as a house repair; for retirement income; or for future purchases (e.g., saving up for a car or electrical goods). Because there are so many categories of saving, decisions regarding saving can be complex. It is therefore important to stand back and spend time managing our finances so we can take a balanced approach to the competing priorities for our money.

As with so many of the decisions we make, there is no right or wrong, and there are no simple answers. The balance of saving, spending and giving will vary from person to person. It will also change over time as our needs, resources and family situation change. As you review your savings, I suggest that you spend some time in prayer, asking for wisdom and acknowledging your accountability to God.

How should we save?

Regardless of how much we choose to save, we need to think through how and where we will save. Christian investors will also want to take ethical considerations into account when making such decisions. For over a hundred years, issues of ethical investment have been gaining prominence, originating from Quaker and Methodist thinking in the nineteenth century.

When we look at ethical investment, we need to consider both positive and negative factors. Positively, we might seek and select companies that:

■ Are environmentally responsible and control pollution

■ Have ethical employment practices

■ Exercise good corporate governance

■ Demonstrate care for the communities in which they operate

On the other hand, negative factors which might dissuade us from investing in a company could include their involvement in selling or promoting:

■ Alcohol or tobacco

■ Armaments and nuclear weapons

■ Animal exploitation

■ Environmentally damaging practices

■ Poor employment practices

■ Gambling

■ Pornography

Ethical factors can influence our decisions in all areas of saving and investment, from choosing current or savings accounts to pension funds and unit or investment trusts, as well as buying shares in individual companies.

Shares in individual companies

The last of these areas is the easiest for an individual investor to screen ethically, since the investment is in a single corporate entity that can easily be researched through the web. Ethical considerations should not be the sole reason for buying shares in individual companies, since they carry a significant element of risk which will not be appropriate for all investors.

Unit and investment trusts and pension funds

The underlying principle of pension funds and unit or investment trusts is that by pooling money from many investors, a sizeable fund can be created that can spread risk across a wider range of investments. It is likely that a proportion of your money will be invested in companies that do not meet your ethical criteria. Quantifying that proportion is very difficult in general funds as most only disclose their largest investments, although the trust's annual report will give some detail of the investments and the underlying policy of the fund manager.

There are now on offer a huge variety of 'ethical' funds to retail investors (you and me). These fall principally into two areas: ethical funds and green funds. Ethical funds apply a range of ethical criteria, both positive and negative, such as the ones listed above. There are also green or environmental funds, which invest in companies whose products and services contribute directly to improving our stewardship of the environment. What is important is that you are happy with the criteria for investment.

Over 400,000 individuals invest over £6 billion in these ethical funds. This is in addition to the significant amount of money invested according to ethical policies by churches and other institutions. There is a huge choice of funds, with over 75 different funds open to retail investors. This has grown six-fold over the last ten years following an increased demand for ethical choices, and the scale of investment in ethical funds is starting to have a significant impact on boardroom thinking.

While a fund is not a good investment solely because it describes itself as ethical, the overall performance of ethical funds is broadly in line with the market as a whole. But the performance of individual funds does vary greatly. Such funds all choose different companies in which to invest, and wisdom and appropriate advice are essential when selecting an investment.

Savings accounts

Savings accounts are difficult to assess from an ethical perspective, as many of the larger banks operate in broadly similar ways. For those who wish to seek providers that operate differently, there are a number of alternatives. Many of these are based on a mutual, or co-operative, model. There are even specifically Christian providers such as the Kingdom Bank and the Catholic Building Society.

Credit unions offer another co-operative model. Savers can pool their savings in a local scheme to provide low-cost loans to members. They are regulated and authorized by the Financial Services Authority, and, like customers of banks and building societies, members of credit unions are protected by the Financial Services Compensation Scheme.

Investment strategy

While individual investors' situations and their appetites for risk will determine the most appropriate investment for them, we would do well to heed Proverbs 21:5, which reminds us that 'The plans of the diligent lead to profit as surely as haste leads to poverty.'

Responsible savings and investment do require diligence and dedicating time and care to reviewing options and making decisions. We should seek good investments – it is good stewardship to place our money where it will grow, but not at any price. And so we are to be diligent in identifying the investment return we might expect to generate, along with the associated risk, and also in understanding the ethical implications of the investment.

Pause for thought

1. Review the savings part of the worksheet on page 16. How do you feel about your savings assets?

2. Review your monthly savings contributions on the worksheet on page 21. Does this feel about right, too little or too much?

3. What are your ethical criteria? Write them down, as this forces you to be clear on them. Now review how your savings and investments fit with your ethical criteria.

PRINCIPLE 5
Give Generously

As we read the Bible, we encounter our fifth and final principle, which challenges us to give generously. As we saw earlier, our giving is in response to God's grace. The degree to which we give (not only of money, but also of hospitality, time, care, compassion, etc.) reveals something about us, and about how we respond to God's love and grace.

Because this is a book on principles for managing our money, we are focusing on monetary giving. But God also calls us to give generously of our time, our gifts and talents, our homes through hospitality, and our concern for others.

> **PRINCIPLE 5:**
> Give generously.

The parable of the Good Samaritan speaks of at least three dimensions of giving. The Samaritan gives loving care to the injured traveller, putting himself at risk (he did not know if the thieves were still around). He also gives his time, as he journeys more slowly along the road to the inn. Finally, he gives generously of his money, offering to pay whatever is required for the injured man's needs. His generosity is not only in meeting the immediate need, but also in the sacrificial abundance of his provision for the needs of this man.

As we pause to review our giving, we need to remember that it is not just about the amount that we give – it is a much broader challenge than that. We must also consider our priorities, our motivations and where we choose to build up our treasure.

When we give, we engage in a cycle of giving. For we reflect God's amazing generosity to us when we give to those around us. We come back again to David's prayer: 'But who am I, and who are my people, that we should be able to give as generously as this? Everything comes from you, and we have given you only what comes from your hand' (1 Chron. 29:14).

What David is saying could be paraphrased as follows: 'God, you are the sole provider of all that we have. Everything here is a result of your generosity. We recognize that all that we have given, you had previously placed in our hands, and then we took it out of our hands, and put it back in your hands.' It's a circle, or a revolution, of giving.

Paul reminds the Corinthian Christians about generosity: 'Remember this: Whoever sows sparingly will also reap sparingly, and whoever sows generously will also reap generously' (2 Cor. 9:6). In one sense, it's obvious – a farmer who scatters seed generously will have a larger harvest than one who is miserly and plants only a few seeds. So it is with giving. God wants to awaken within us an abundance mentality – that we can give generously, frequently and spontaneously.

The following five characteristics of Christian giving may help us reflect on our generosity. Christian giving should be: 1) a priority; 2) planned; 3) proportionate to our income; 4) sacrificial; and 5) characterized by joy.

First, Christian giving should be a *priority* as we plan our finances. The biblical picture here is 'firstfruits' (Deut. 18:4) – the first and best of the harvest belongs to God. The monthly budget and expenses worksheets on pages 20 and 21 deliberately place giving on the first line of the spending plan. Rather than treating what we give as an afterthought, we should fix the baseline of our giving before we allocate funds to maintain our standard of living.

Second, Christian giving should be *planned*. If we do not make conscious decisions about how much to give and establish direct debits or standing orders, we are likely to give less. Yet it is also good to retain some spontaneity – we should give in response to the needs that we find, just as the Good Samaritan responded generously to the needs of the traveller he encountered.

One way of doing this is to make a regular standing order to a Sovereign or Charities Aid Foundation (CAF) account. It is like a bank account dedicated to your giving to churches and charities. You make regular deposits by direct debit and, if you are a UK taxpayer, HMRC adds tax paid at the basic rate of income tax. You can make regular payments to churches and charities from this type of account, and you also receive regular statements and a charity 'cheque' book to make one-off payments whenever you like. In this way you can give spontaneously when you encounter a need, yet you have already set aside money to be given, and it is ready waiting. Nearly 100,000 people already use these kinds of accounts.

Third, Christian giving is *proportionate*. Many churches teach tithing, or giving 10% of one's income. The Church of England recommends that our initial target should be to give 5% of our net income to the church, and to give a further 5% to other causes we wish to support. Some who are wealthy may find that they are able to give at a far higher level.

Proportionate giving forms the base of our giving, rather than the limit. One of the drawbacks of tithing is that it can be seen in a legalistic, reluctant way – 10% for God, 90% for me. This kind of attitude, of course, belies the first principle of the Money Revolution – that God is the ultimate owner of all that we have. Thus individual needs and causes may move us to respond above the level of our initial proportionate giving.

The worksheet on the next page will help you to review your base for giving; who you have been supporting; and how much you have given. Then you can calculate how your regular, planned giving (monthly or annual) compares with your income. You should include regular payments to a Sovereign or CAF account. In general, you should not include ad hoc responses to individual appeals, which are expressions of generosity over and above our planned regular gifts.

Fourth, Christian giving should be *sacrificial*. Jesus observed a poor widow putting two small coins into the temple offertory. Jesus did not leap to his feet, anxious to intercept a woman who had misunderstood the tithe by giving all she had, to tell her she should hold onto the second coin. Rather than pointing out that just one of the coins would represent 50% of her income, and that would be more than enough to fulfil the law, he recognizes and praises her generosity. The proportionate giving represents a base of giving, but we are called to be generous in responding to needs as we come across them, above and beyond that which is demanded by proportionate giving.

Paul records the Macedonian Christians giving 'as much as they were able [proportionately], and even beyond their ability [sacrificially], they urgently pleaded with us for the privilege of sharing in this service to the Lord's people' (2 Cor. 8:3–4).

Bishop Jack Nicholls, Bishop of Sheffield, once said, 'Our generosity is measured not by what we give, but by what we have left when we have given.' The gift of the poor widow was of lower financial value than the gifts of those who had preceded her, but her gift represented far greater generosity. One of the surprising statistics we encounter when we look at giving levels between different areas of the country is that it is very often

Giving Grid

Frequency	Cause Supported	Monthly Amount
Monthly		
Quarterly or Six Monthly		
Annual		
Total Monthly Planned Giving (A)		
Total Monthly Income (B)		
Giving as a % of Income (A/B) x 100		

those in poorer areas who show greater generosity, giving at proportionate levels of income which are higher than those living in wealthier areas.

Finally, our Christian giving should be *joyful*. We should give with gladness in our hearts, knowing that the money that we give leads to God's work being done – furthering the mission of the church, ministering to the sick, or relieving famine or poverty. When Paul talks about giving he uses the Greek *hilarion*, a word close to our word hilarious. The idea is that the giver overflows with joy at the work that can result from being able to give back what God has provided.

Like the Vikings who wanted to hold their sword arm above the waters of baptism, giving our wallets and our financial resources to God is a step of faith. But it is not one we should take reluctantly, or as a result of guilt. Rather, it is to be done joyfully and cheerfully. As we reflect on God's ultimate ownership of all that we have, and the different decisions we might make in the light of that knowledge, we come to realize just how much treasure we can store up in heaven.

We close this chapter by considering our motivation for, and the consequences of, our giving. Some churches have taught a 'prosperity gospel' – that those who give will be given greater financial wealth in this life. This teaching is based on extrapolating passages such as the prayer of Jabez (1 Chron. 4:9–10), or Proverbs 11:24–25: 'One person gives freely, yet gains even more; another withholds unduly, but comes to poverty. A generous person will prosper; whoever refreshes others will be refreshed.'

Let us remember that in God's economy, financial wealth is not necessarily the yardstick we should use to assess God's blessing. Yes, we can be assured that there will be blessing for those who give generously. Yes, we can trust God to provide for our needs. But this will not necessarily equate to earthly riches. Our giving should not be motivated by any prospect of receiving wealth in this life. Rather, we should maintain a clear focus of heart, mind and motive on heaven.

In Proverbs 11:24–25, which we read above, the one who unduly withholds may maintain great earthly riches, yet in the fullness of time will lack spiritual blessings. Verse 25 provides a parallelism: 'a generous person' is, in Hebrew, 'the soul of blessing'. When we bless others, we ourselves may come to know God's blessing. The second line uses the metaphor of providing water for the thirsty, for our own spiritual refreshment. Christian experience is that God does provide for the needs of those who are generous, but that is a far different claim to that of the prosperity gospel.

Application **Why Every Christian Should Make a Will**

For over five hundred years, the church has encouraged Christians in England to make a will. When Archbishop Cranmer wrote the first English Prayer Book he instructed clergy to remind parishioners to keep their wills up to date while they were still in good health, for their own peace of mind as well as to help their executors.

Every year many thousands of people die 'intestate' (without leaving a will). This can cause unnecessary complications for their families and friends, and it often means their wishes cannot be carried out. If you die in England or Wales without a valid will, the courts will decide what happens to your possessions. The Family Division of the court follows strict legal rules that do not make provision for partners who are not married, or friends or churches or charities.

As part of our Christian stewardship, or our responsibility for that with which we have been entrusted, we should make a will and encourage others to do the same. The five principles of the Money Revolution not only relate to the whole of our lives, but they can also make an impact on what we leave behind. Making a will is part of active stewardship and allows us to demonstrate generosity in our provision for our families and loved ones, as well as for the causes that are important to us.

Making a will is also an important part of our responsibility to God as stewards of everything with which he has provided us. When we make a will, we consciously decide what will happen to our wealth. Very seldom do we take such an overview, and our wills are written summaries of what we hold to be important in our lives.

Things change over the course of our lives, and it's important to review and make appropriate revisions to our wills at regular intervals. The arrival of children or grandchildren, changes in family circumstances, moving house, and many other factors may cause you to want to change your will. Out-of-date wills (e.g., with old addresses) can cause unnecessary complications, distress and expense for the surviving family and friends.

Keeping wills reasonably up to date is not only sound financial management, but good Christian discipleship. Most Christians pray about how much they will regularly give to their local church and other Christian agencies, and when writing our wills we can also pray about how we allocate the assets God has given us on earth.

I suggest that you make a note to review your will every five years (e.g., in years with significant birthdays ending in a '5' or '0').

Making a will is often a simpler and less expensive process than many people imagine. Because a will needs to be legally valid, however, it is important to use a professional rather than relying on a DIY kit from a stationer's.

Because we were created to be naturally creative, it's easy to think up reasons to delay making a will. Some of the common ones include:

'I'm too young to think about dying.' Unfortunately tragic accidents do happen. Do you really want everything you own to be distributed according to a fixed legal formula? It is particularly important to write or amend your will if you get married or start a civil partnership, and to appoint potential guardians when you have children.

'I don't have anything to leave.' But you probably do own a few treasured items that you would like to be passed on to particular relatives or friends. Without a will they will be sold (probably very cheaply), and any money will be used to pay legal costs or distributed according to an official formula.

'I don't have the time.' Organizing a will is straightforward and only takes a few hours of your time. It will save your family and friends much more time, trouble and expense after your death. It will also provide you with an opportunity to take stock of your life and possessions, and decide on future priorities.

'It's too expensive to make a will.' Straightforward wills cost less than £100 from expert solicitors, and you may find much less expensive deals. If you are elderly and on a very low income you may be able to benefit from Legal Aid. Some charities subsidize wills for certain groups of people (e.g., those over 55).

'Thinking about dying makes me uncomfortable.' The old adage says, 'There are only two certainties in life – death and taxes.' If we care for those we love, we need to prepare for what is bound to happen at some unknown time in the future. It may be of help to consider the eternal hope that we have as Christians. The arrangements that we make in our wills are only to cover an interim period.

'I haven't decided how my estate should be divided yet.' Your wishes (and the needs of your family and friends) will probably evolve over time as your circumstances change. But you can easily work out an appropriate sharing of your estate if you were to die unexpectedly in the next few months. After that, if you review your will every five years or when major life events happen (e.g., marriage or co-habitation, birth of a child or grandchild, death of a beneficiary) you can make simple adjustments as necessary.

'My partner will get it all anyway.' Not necessarily. Married spouses may not get everything – especially if there are children or the estate includes a property. Partners who are not legally married (or do not have a legally registered civil partnership) may get nothing.

'Everyone knows what I want to happen.' Without a written will that has been properly witnessed, the courts will decide how any estate is to be distributed according to a fixed legal formula that almost certainly will differ from what you really want.

How can I make a will?

The best way to make a will is to see a solicitor who is trained in all aspects of the law and tax and is insured to protect his/her clients. If you don't know a solicitor, ask your family and friends for a recommendation. Not all solicitors are equally expert in all areas of the law, and you should seek one who is experienced in writing wills (called a probate solicitor) rather than one who, for example, specializes in property and conveyancing. The Law Society website (www.lawsociety.org.uk) contains a searchable database of solicitors specializing in probate. Other organizations you might find helpful are the Society of Trust and Estate Professionals (www.step.org) and the Institute of Professional Willwriters (www.ipw.org.uk). The IPW is a body that provides professional standards for willwriters who are not qualified solicitors.

As we have seen, making or revising a will need not be expensive, and you should be able to get a quote before you engage a solicitor. You can get a pack that will help you do this from several charities, including the Church of England's information line: 08445 870875.

Preparing to make a will

Before visiting a solicitor, it may be helpful to think through the wishes you want to express in your will. You can download a copy of a worksheet from the Money Revolution website to take with you when you visit your solicitor. If you have previously made a will or added a codicil, you should also take that with you.

1. **Your details**: Your full name, address and postcode and telephone number.

2. **Identify what you own and what you owe** using the worksheet on page 16.

3. **Your executors**. You will need to decide who you want to carry out your will. Most wills appoint one or two executors, and there is a maximum of four. You can include your solicitor, bank or accountant, but your estate will be charged for their professional work. You should make sure that at least one of your executors is likely to survive you. Your solicitor will need to know their full name, address and telephone number.

4. **Young children**. If you have dependent children it is advisable to appoint a guardian to look after them until they are at least 18 years old. You should ask for the potential guardian's agreement before appointing them. Your solicitor will need their full name, address and telephone number.

5. **Specific gifts or legacies**. In your will you can nominate specific items (e.g., heirlooms, paintings, jewellery) that you want to leave to family, friends or charities. You should describe them in some detail to avoid any future misunderstandings. Your solicitor will need the full names, addresses and telephone numbers of those to whom you would like to leave items.

6. **Gifts of money**. You should make a list of any set sums of money you wish to leave to people and/or to your church or charities. These are called pecuniary legacies. Again, your solicitor will need the full names, addresses and telephone numbers of those to whom you would like to leave such gifts.

7. **Sharing the remainder of your estate**. List the people and/or church or charities that you would like to share the remainder or residue of your estate once all of the above legacies have been made. These gifts are called residuary legacies.

8. **Other instructions and requests for executors**. Sometimes it may be sensible to write a side letter to your executors setting out other non-binding preferences (e.g., your wishes for your funeral, or what you would like to happen to any pets you may have at the time of your death). The letter should be stored with your formal will, but not attached to it.

9. **Questions**. Finally, you should also make a note of any particular questions you may have for your solicitor or other professional advisers.

Application **Getting through the Eye of the Needle**

After Jesus had met with the rich young ruler in Matthew 19, he talked with his disciples about how difficult it is for the rich to make sure their wealth doesn't get in the way of their salvation. Jesus compared it to getting a camel, their largest animal, through the eye of a needle. 'Who then can be saved?' asked the disciples. Jesus responded, 'with God all things are possible.' It is not easy seeking to apply these principles in a prosperous society. In the parable of the talents, the servant who is active in his stewardship of his master's possessions is the one who is commended.

Wealth and possessions are both a blessing and a challenge. God has richly blessed us, and we need to practise good habits of stewardship to make sure those riches never occupy too large a place in our lives. In this chapter, then, we examine how we might adopt such habits and develop our stewardship further.

The first principle of the Money Revolution is that everything comes from God. We are merely looking after the resources God has given us. Just as we choose to give our hearts and minds to him, we are also called to give our wallets and financial resources to God.

 Action: If you are willing to commit yourself to the Money Revolution principles, pray for God's help in following them through and put the card into your wallet as an act of commitment, possibly placing it in front of your credit card. While it will get in the way of quickly withdrawing your card, it will also act as a more prominent reminder.

Principle 2 reminds us to be active stewards. As such, we need to take an overview of our budget and spending patterns periodically, as well as being wise on individual purchase decisions.

Action: This book may have led you to review your finances more thoroughly than you have done for a while. It is good to undertake a thorough 'budget review' at least once a year. Why not put the next date in your diary now?

Principle 3 encourages us to build the gap between our income and our expenditure so that we can free up money we can use to further God's work. As you have worked through the exercises in this book, you will hopefully have identified several areas where you could reduce your outgoings.

Pause for a moment and spend some time thanking God for his generous provision for you, and ask God for wisdom to identify opportunities where you could increase your income or reduce your expenditure. Then see if you can list five specific actions that will increase the gap between your income and your expenditures. Where possible, try to focus on areas of regular spending rather than one-off purchases. These principles are designed to encourage good habits, rather than being a one-off cost-saving exercise.

Even if you can't think of five areas, working on one or two initially can make a real difference, and you can see if you can find some more things to work on in a few months' time.

Action:
Opportunities to Build the Gap

Opportunity   Financial Impact £

1. ....

2. ....

3. ....

4. ....

5. ....

Total impact per year...........................   £............................

Examples might be reviewing your regular monthly subscriptions (e.g., gym, internet, TV) to see if there are alternatives which better suit your usage patterns; considering switching mortgage or loans to ones with lower interest rates; reviewing how much food you throw away, etc.

The final two principles of the Money Revolution encourage us to focus on building treasure in heaven. We do this through our generosity in giving our money, our time and our hearts and minds to God's work. Review the 'Giving Grid' you completed on page 52 and consider what changes you would like to make to your current patterns of giving. You might like to write down a long-term aim, as well as some shorter-term stepping stones to help you get there.

Action:

My long-term goal for giving generously is that I will give at least ....% of my income.

My first two steps to build towards this are:

1 ....

2 ....

Here is a short checklist of action items resulting from the application of the five principles of the Money Revolution.

1. What else could you be doing to take your stewardship of the planet seriously? Review the tips provided on page 35 and consider which you will put into action.

2. Having reflected on your long-term savings and pensions plans, do you consider them to be appropriate? You might want to consult an Independent Financial Adviser to help you with this. If you want to talk with a Christian adviser, the Association of Christian Financial Advisers has a website listing their members at www.christianfinancialadvisers.org.uk.

3. Have you made a will? If you do have a will, does it need to be reviewed? Does it reflect your current wishes and situation?

Becoming a money revolutionary

I hope this book has convinced you that how we in the UK handle the relative wealth and prosperity that God has blessed us with is an issue of faith, justice and responsibility. Our lifestyle and spending decisions proclaim our values and faith as much as our words and actions. Yet this is not an issue that has been well taught. Indeed, you may be encountering a Christian perspective on some of the areas discussed in this book for the first time.

In addition to applying the Money Revolution principles to your life, there are several things that you could do to help others benefit from these principles. Here are two possibilities:

1. Be a sponsor. Special bulk discounts are available for this workbook. See www.themoneyrevolution.net or contact your local Christian bookshop. Consider buying enough copies to give to your church's planned givers, to help them benefit from this teaching. This could be done anonymously through your Gift Aid secretary as a thank you from the church.

2. There is a growing network of volunteers run by Stewardship, who seek to encourage the principles put forward in this book. You could consider becoming a volunteer or church contact. The roles of the volunteers vary to suit individual skills, preferences and commitments: leading study courses, making presentations or speaking in local churches. Some are skilled debt advisors and many are trained as personal budget coaches to assist people in preparing realistic and workable budgets. All volunteers are committed to promoting wise and biblical thinking about money. The vision is for Christians and their churches to reflect the generosity of God in the joy of their giving and to be faithful stewards of all that God has given. To find out more visit www.stewardship.org.uk.

What If?
The Money Revolution

The ideas presented in this book might revolutionize your thinking about your personal finances. It's possible that they might lead you to reduce your spending and increase the money you are able to give. It may be that you gain a fresh perspective on how everything fits together – saving and spending, giving and lifestyle.

However, the Money Revolution will only really gather momentum when Christians all over the nation start living by these principles. If all regular churchgoers in the UK could save an additional 5% of their incomes, and give that money to Christian work, then an additional thousand million pounds a year, or one billion pounds, would be invested in God's economy.

Just imagine for a moment what that could accomplish if the money was divided five ways . . .

■ Just one-fifth of the money generated would enable our churches to fund 10,000 more full-time community workers called to work with our children and young people, the old and the disadvantaged.

■ Two-fifths might contribute to the fight to eradicate poverty and ill health. This share would generate new funding exceeding the current income of Christian Aid, CAFOD, Oxfam, World Vision, CMS and Tearfund combined.

■ A further fifth might provide the start-up capital to initiate projects such as centres for refugees and asylum seekers, debt counselling centres, community cafes and other projects. If the average investment required to initiate each project was £100,000, then 2,000 such projects could be funded each year.

■ A final portion could be given to our churches, to enable local ministry and mission to grow and prosper, without the need for penny pinching. The average church might gain around £5,000 per year to help remove lack of finances as a barrier to many visionary ideas and projects.

And along the way we would probably . . .

- Reduce our consumption of products we don't really need, helping us resist the challenges of consumerism.

- Harm the environment less by being better stewards of the planet.

- Reduce or eliminate our personal debt, providing testimony to others that it is possible to live within our resources.

- Become more personally involved in the causes we support and discover the joy of generous giving.

That would indeed be a Money Revolution!